CW01309623

RAILWAYS OF PORTUGAL
by Peter J Green

Published by Mainline & Maritime Ltd, 3 Broadleaze, Upper Seagry, near Chippenham, SN15 5EY
Tel: 01275 845012   www.mainlineandmaritime.co.uk   orders@mainlineandmaritime.co.uk
ISBN: 978-1-900340-81-6 Printed in the UK © Mainline & Maritime Ltd, & Author 2021
All rights reserved. No part of this publication may be reproduced by any process without the prior written permission of the publisher. The contents of this book were originally self-published by the Author using the Blurb platform under the title *Railways of Portugal: 40 Years of Change.* They are reproduced here with the permission of the Author.

Front Cover: English Electric no. 1810 shunts a parcels van at Barreiro Station. 17th March 1992.

Back Cover: Between June and October, CP run steam-hauled excursion trains from Régua to Tua. Here, Henschel 2-8-4T no. 0186 of 1925 is pictured shunting at Tua, during one of the excursions. 15th September 2007.

Paul Dorney

Above: An unidentified Bombardier diesel locomotive heads a train of bagged cement from Vila Nova de Gaia to Darque, across Durrães Viaduct on the Minho line. The Minho line runs from Porto to Valença do Minho, on the Spanish border. 10th September 2008.

Paul Dorney

CONTENTS

Introduction..3
The Steam Era Railway in Northern Portugal, the Douro Valley, and around Porto and Sernada do Vouga, in the 1970s..4
The Modern Era in Northern Portugal.........................48
The Modern Era along the Douro Valley Line and its Metre Gauge Branches...52
The Modern Era in the Porto Area...............................67
The Modern Era in Central Portugal............................74
The Modern Era in Southern Portugal......................102
A Visit to Entroncamento..136
Trams in Portugal...138
A Final Look..141
Appendix 1: Locomotive Details................................142
Appendix 2: Railway Routes in Portugal..................143

REFERENCES

- Portuguese Railways website; https://www.cp.pt/passageiros/en/
- The European Railway Server; http://www.railfaneurope.net/
- A Guide to Portuguese Railways by David Clough, Martin Beckett and Michael Hunt. Published in 1991 by Fearless Publications.
- Railway Holiday in Portugal by D.W. Winkworth. Published in 1968 by David and Charles ISBN 7153 4301 7.
- Continental Railway Handbooks, Spain and Portugal by D. Trevor Rowe. Published in 1970 by Ian Allan ISBN 7110 0176 6.
- French and Iberian Steam compiled by T. W. J. Auty. Published by the North Eastern Locomotive Preservation Group in 1972.
- Various issues of Today's Railways, Europe magazine. Published monthly by Platform 5 Publishing.

Murals, produced from tiles, decorate the railway station at Régua. 18th September 1993.

INTRODUCTION

Portugal has been a popular destination for railway enthusiasts for many years. In the late 1960s and into the 1970s, British enthusiasts travelled around Europe and farther afield, looking for a substitute for the working steam that had disappeared from the main line in their own country in 1968. In Portugal they found a beautiful country, very different from Britain at that time, a friendly reception from the railway staff, and most important of all, splendid steam locomotives working on both the broad gauge and the charming metre gauge systems in the northern part of the country.

Regular steam working in Portugal ended in the 1970s, but, by then, many enthusiasts were beginning to take more of an interest in the modern railway scene. In Portugal, there was an interesting fleet of locomotives and railcars, many of them old, and the Douro Valley in the north, with its metre gauge railways, became popular with visiting enthusiasts once more. The Lisboa area, Barreiro and the south, as well as other parts of the country, also saw many visitors. Despite the various modernisation schemes around the country, this has continued until the present day.

For the enthusiast with broader interests, the old tramcars that operated in Lisboa and Porto were a further attraction. Some historic trams are still operated for tourists.

Caminhos de Ferro Portugueses (Comboios de Portugal since 2009) or CP is the state owned company which previously operated freight and passenger trains in Portugal. The infrastructure is now owned by Infraestruturas de Portugal and the freight operation was sold to MSC Logistics. Most of the railway system is broad gauge of 1,668 mm. or 5 ft $5^{21}/_{32}$ in. and totals around 2,600 km. Much of it is now electrified at 25 kV 50 Hz AC, with overhead catenary. The 26 km. Estoril railway, electrified in 1926, uses a 1.5 kV DC overhead system.

Following closures, little now remains of the metre gauge railways. The lines from Espinho and Aveiro to Sernada do Vouga and the Metro de Mirandela, totalling around 100 km., are all that are left, while the Porto Metro runs on the old metre gauge trackbed from Porto Trindade to Póvoa de Varzim.

The modern railway in Portugal has seen spreading electrification, new and rebuilt stations including Lisboa Oriente, a railway bridge over the Tagus largely replacing the old CP ferries, new and faster passenger trains, and private operators running freight trains on its network. But Portugal also has an eye on its railway's past, and the National Railway Museum was opened at Entroncamento in 2007, the building being in the style of an old steam roundhouse.

There are also other small museums around the country and a large number of steam locomotives still exist, although many are now in derelict condition. At least there is hope while they are still there.

My first visit to Portugal was in 1972, a package holiday to Póvoa de Varzim, arranged to see the steam operation and something of the country in general. This was only my third trip abroad. Regular journeys were made into Porto by train, usually behind one of the big Henschel 2-8-2 tank engines, often arriving rather dirtier than when I set off! Visits were also made during the 1990s when, apart from steam no longer operating, the general nature of the railway had not changed too much.

Producing this book has been an interesting and enjoyable process and trying to make the most of the images from deteriorating colour slides has been just one of the challenges. My intention has been to show something of the changing railway scene over a period of around forty years, commencing in the early 1970s. I hope that this objective, at least in part, has been achieved.

I would like to express my thanks to those people who have contributed photographs and provided general assistance in the production of this book. In particular, thanks are due to Paul Dorney, Val Brown, Paul Bryson, Jackie Green and Steve Turner.

The photographs in this book are my own, except where otherwise credited.

Peter J. Green
Worcester, England
2021

THE STEAM ERA RAILWAY IN NORTHERN PORTUGAL, THE DOURO VALLEY, AND AROUND PORTO AND SERNADA DO VOUGA, IN THE 1970S

2-6-4T no. 079 makes smoke for the photographer as it takes water at Braga locomotive depot. Note the 1401 class diesel in blue livery in the background. 6th August 1972.

Jackie Green

Hartmann 0-4-0T no. 002 of 1881 runs on to the turntable at Contumil locomotive depot, near Porto. Contumil was the main steam locomotive depot in Portugal at this time. 10th August 1972.

Jackie Green

Preserved Beyer, Peacock and Co. 0-6-2T no. 013 of 1889 stands next to 2-8-0 no. 705 and 2-6-4T no. 084 at Contumil locomotive depot. No. 013 is now stored at Lagos. 10th August 1972.

Jackie Green

Withdrawn Henschel 4-6-0 no. 283 is viewed through the window of a derelict coach at Vila Nova de Gaia. 11th August 1972.
Jackie Green

The 191 km. broad gauge Douro Valley line, from Ermesinde to Barca d'Alva near the Spanish border, with its metre gauge branches, was a popular destination for railway enthusiasts in the steam era and after. The metre gauge lines, which ran from Livração to Arco do Baúlhe (Linha do Tâmega), Régua to Chaves (Linha do Corgo), Tua to Bragança (Linha do Tua), and Pocinho to Duas Igrejas (Linha do Sabor), have now all closed, except for a short section of the Linha do Tua, the Metro de Mirandela, which runs from Carvalhais to Mirandela and is operated by two modern railcars. The principal locomotive depot along the Douro Valley was at Régua. Here, Henschel inside cylinder 4-6-0 no. 281 of 1910 stands on the turntable at Régua loco depot. 15th August 1972.

Jackie Green

Henschel inside cylinder 4-6-0 no. 281 stands at Régua station. 15th August 1972.

Jackie Green

Pocinho, 175 km. from Porto on the Douro Valley line, was the junction for the metre gauge line to Duas Igrejas. Metre gauge yard pilot 0-6-0T no. E54, built by Maschinenfabrik Esslingen in 1889, is pictured shunting at Pocinho. September 1974.

Paul Bryson

Metre gauge Hohenzollern 0-6-0T no. E41 of 1904 at Pocinho. September 1974.

Paul Bryson

The metre gauge railway system, based on Porto, consisted of lines from Porto Trindade station to Póvoa de Varzim (30 km.) and Lousado (31 km.), as well as lines from Póvoa de Varzim to Lousado (36 km.) and Lousado to Guimarães and Fafe (52 km.). The principal locomotive depot for the system was Boa Vista which was located next to Avenida da França station, 3 km. from Trindade. All the lines are now closed apart from the section from Trindade to Póvoa de Varzim, which forms part of the Porto Metro. Henschel 0-4-4-0T no. E167 is pictured at Boa Vista locomotive depot. Ten of these Mallet tank locomotives were built between 1905 and 1908. Note the Allan railcar in the background. August 1972

Paul Bryson

The original terminus of the Porto metre gauge system was Boa Vista station, adjacent to Boa Vista locomotive depot. It was still standing in 1972 and, although no longer a passenger station, freight wagons were sometimes stored alongside its platforms. 7th August 1972.

Jackie Green

Aveiro station is located on the Porto to Lisboa broad gauge line, 67 km. from Porto. It is also the terminus of the metre gauge line from Sernada do Vouga. Tiles are used to form attractive murals showing local scenes on many station buildings in Portugal. Aveiro station was a fine example of the art and is pictured here in 1972. The station was rebuilt around the year 2000 and, while the original station building, complete with its tiles, was retained, it is not now part of the station operation. 13th August 1972.

Jackie Green

Sernada do Vouga was the junction for the metre gauge lines to Aveiro (35 km.), and Espinho (62 km.), both on the broad gauge main line from Porto to Lisboa. A third metre gauge line ran from Sernada do Vouga to Viseu (79 km.) and on to Santa Comba Dão (50 km.). Only the lines to Aveiro and Espinho remain today. Both the principal locomotive depot and the works for the system were located at Sernada do Vouga. Petrol railcar no. ME54, built at Sernada in the 1940s, is on the turntable at Sernada after arrival from Espinho. After turning, it will continue to Viseu. 13th August 1972.

Jackie Green

2-6-4T no. 079 takes water at Braga locomotive depot. Twenty eight of these locomotives, nos. 070 to 097, were built by the CP Lisboa workshops, the Swiss Locomotive and Machine Works, and Henschel and Sohn for the Portuguese railways, between 1916 and 1944. 6th August 1972.

Preserved broad gauge 2-2-2ST CP no. 02049, built by Fairbairn of Leeds in 1854, stands inside the loco shed at Braga. This locomotive is ex Minho and Douro Railway no. 13. 6th August 1972.

Henschel 4-6-0 no. 281 of 1910 departs from Régua station with a mixed train to the east. 15th August 1972.

Inside and outside cylinder Henschel 4-6-0s stand at Régua, next to the turntable. The locomotives are no. 286 of 1910, left, and no. 292 of 1913. 15th August 1972.

The metre gauge Linha do Corgo ran for 97 km. from Régua to Chaves. The motive power for the line was the class of 2-4-6-0 Mallet tank engines built by Henschel between 1911 and 1923. In this view, Mallet 2-4-6-0T no. E215 departs from Régua with a Corgo line train. 15th August 1972.

The 105 km. long, metre gauge Linha do Sabor ran from Pocinho, 175 km. from Porto on the Douro Valley line, to Duas Igrejas. The line was worked by Mallet 2-4-6-0Ts. Here, no. E216 is serviced at Pocinho, next to broad gauge Henschel 4-6-0 no. 292. Note the dual gauge track. September 1974.

Paul Bryson

The Henschel inside cylinder 4-6-0s were particularly fine looking locomotives, reminiscent of some British designs, as can be seen in this splendid 1974 portrait. Here, 4-6-0 no. 282 of 1910 pauses at Pocinho with a mixed train to the west. September 1974.

Paul Bryson

Sixteen 2-8-0 locomotives were built by Schwartzkopf and the North British Locomotive Co., originally for the Minho Douro Railway, between 1912 and 1924. These locomotives were four-cylinder compounds with bar frames. Here, one of the North British locomotives, withdrawn CP no. 751, is pictured at Contumil. 10th August 1972.

Nineteen two-cylinder simple 2-8-0 locomotives, with plate frames, were built by Schwartzkopf and the North British Locomotive Co. between 1912 and 1921. Eleven of these locomotives remained active in 1972. Here, CP no. 717, built by North British in 1921, stands under the wires at Contumil. 10th August 1972.

2-6-4T no. 070, built by the CP Lisboa workshops in 1944, takes water at Contumil locomotive depot. 10th August 1972.

Société Alsacienne de Constructions Mécaniques, Belfort, 0-6-0 no. 167 (Works no. 4074 of 1888) stands in the line of withdrawn locomotives at Contumil depot. 10th August 1972.

Shed pilot Hartmann 0-4-0T no. 002 of 1881 takes water at Contumil locomotive depot. 10th August 1972.

Porto Trindade station was the terminus of the metre gauge railway system in the north. Today, all that remains of the system is the line from Trindade to Póvoa de Varzim, which forms part of the Porto Metro. Here, Esslingen 2-6-0T no. E85 of 1886 runs past the signal box at Porto Trindade station. 5th August 1972.

The main locomotive depot for the metre gauge railway system, which started from Porto Trindade, was at Boa Vista which was located next to Avenida da França station, 3 km. from Trindade. Maschinenfabrik Esslingen 2-6-0T no. E103 of 1907 shunts at this depot. 7th August 1972.

Esslingen 2-6-0T no. E83 of 1886 moves off the shed. No. E101 is on the right, and an Allan railcar, with a trailer, is in the background, on the left. 7th August 1972.

Withdrawn Esslingen 0-6-0T no. E53 of 1889 at Boa Vista locomotive depot, next to the remains of former Vale of Vouga motorised goods van no. ME21, built at Sernada do Vouga in 1944/5. Note the washing hanging up to dry inside the cab! 7th August 1972.

Decauville no. E93 of 1910 at Boa Vista shed. 7th August 1972.

A smoky scene at Boa Vista locomotive depot with Esslingen 2-6-0T no. E103 of 1907, left, and Henschel 2-8-2T no. E142 of 1931. 7th August 1972.

A general view of Boa Vista locomotive depot. Locomotives visible include nos. E142, left, and E103. The closed Boa Vista station, the original terminus of the Porto metre gauge system, can be seen to the right of the photograph, between the depot building and the water tower. 7th August 1972.

Esslingen 2-6-0T no. E103 of 1907 backs down on to a rake of coaches at Senhora da Hora, before drawing forward into the station with a short working to Porto Trindade. 9th August 1972.

Esslingen 2-6-0T no. E114 of 1908 starts its train away from Porto Trindade station. 15th August 1972.

Henschel Mallet 0-4-4-0T no. E165 of 1908 shunts in the afternoon sunshine at Póvoa de Varzim. The line to Famalicão and Lousado is on the right. c1970.

Paul Dorney Collection

Henschel 0-4-4-0T no. E161 of 1905 and 2-8-2T no. E144 stand in front of the loco shed at Póvoa de Varzim. 17th August 1972.

Esslingen 2-6-0T no. E102 is turned at Póvoa de Varzim, after arriving from Lousado. 18th August 1972.

Four large metre gauge 2-8-2Ts, nos. E141- E144, were supplied by Henschel to the Portuguese railways (Companhia do Caminhode Ferro do Valle do Vouga) in 1931. By 1972, all were allocated to Porto Boa Vista shed and were used mainly on the Porto to Póvoa de Varzim and Lousado trains.

Henschel 2-8-2T no. E142 of 1931 is prepared for its next duty, alongside the loco shed at Póvoa de Varzim. 5th August 1972.

Henschel 2-8-2T no. E144 of 1931 waits to depart from Póvoa de Varzim with a train to Porto Trindade. August 1972.
Paul Bryson

Local people look on as Esslingen 2-6-0T no. E102 of 1907 approaches Póvoa de Varzim with a train from Lousado. 18th August 1972.

Esslingen 2-6-0T no. E102 of 1907 stands next to the turntable at Póvoa de Varzim with a train to Lousado. 18th August 1972.

Henschel 2-8-2T no. E143 of 1931 crosses the Ponte do Ave at Vila do Conde with a train from Póvoa de Varzim to Porto Trindade. c1970.

Paul Dorney collection

Famalicão looking north. Metre gauge 2-8-2T no. E142, with a train from the Póvoa de Varzim line, and broad gauge 2-6-4T no. 072, with a train from the north, stand on the opposite sides of the island platform at Famalicão. The metre and standard gauge lines ran together from Famalicão, southward through Lousado, to Trofa, where the metre gauge line to Porto Trindade diverged. 6th August 1972.

Sernada do Vouga was the junction for the metre gauge lines to Aveiro (35 km.), and Espinho (62 km.), both on the broad gauge main line from Porto to Lisboa. A third metre gauge line ran from Sernada do Vouga to Viseu (79 km.) and on to Santa Comba Dão (50 km.). Only the lines to Aveiro and Espinho remain today. Both the principal locomotive depot and the works for the system were at Sernada do Vouga.

Upper: A general view of the station and locomotive depot, looking east.
13th August 1972.

Lower: A petrol railcar approaches from the east. 13th August 1972.

Esslingen 2-6-0T no. E84 of 1886 shunts at Sernada do Vouga. 13th August 1972.

Henschel 2-8-2T no. E131 stands at Sernada do Vouga with the 14.10 to Viseu. 2-6-0T no. E95 attaches an extra coach to the rear of the train. 13th August 1972.

Decauville 2-6-0T no. E95 of 1910 crosses the viaduct over the River Vouga, as it approaches Sernada do Vouga with a train from Aveiro. Note the siding running down to the river. 13th August 1972.

Henschel 2-8-2T no. E131 of 1924 and Borsig 4-6-0T no. E122 of 1908 at Sernada do Vouga locomotive depot. 13th August 1972.

THE MODERN ERA IN NORTHERN PORTUGAL

Co-Co Bombardier diesel no. 1965 of 1973 shunts empty timber wagons at Valença do Minho. After loading in the sidings, the timber will go to one of the Altri or Soporcel paper plants. Note the semaphore signals to the right of the locomotive and the railcar in the station. 17th September 2008.

Paul Dorney

English Electric no. 1402 stands at Viana do Castelo with the 10-40 to Porto São Bento. No. 1441 is on the right. 9th July 2001.
Paul Dorney

A steam era scene at Nine that is spoilt only by the modern diesel multiple unit. An 0450 series unit stands in front of the old steam shed, next to a semaphore signal. Note the old water crane on the left. The 0450 series diesel multiple units of 1999 were modernised and refurbished 0400 series units, which were built by Sorefame in 1965/66. 16th September 2005.

Paul Dorney

Bombardier no. 1964 runs southward along the Atlantic coast, near Ãncora, with a container train from Vigo in Spain. 19th September 2002.

Paul Dorney

THE MODERN ERA ALONG THE DOURO VALLEY LINE AND ITS METRE GAUGE BRANCHES

An unidentified English Electric 14xx diesel runs alongside the Douro River near Barqueiros with the 14.50 Porto São Bento to Pocinho. 25th March 2005.

Paul Dorney

On the Douro Valley line, English Electric Bo-Bo no. 1436, built by Sorefame in 1967, leaves the tunnel west of Godim with a train from Godim cement terminal to Vila Nova de Gaia. 13th July 2001.

Paul Dorney

English Electric no. 1409 stands at Régua with the 14.35 Porto São Bento to Pocinho. Ten of these Bo-Bo diesel-electric locomotives, nos 1401 to 1410, were constructed at Vulcan Foundry for CP in 1966. A further fifty seven, nos. 1411 to 1467, were built by Sorefame under licence from English Electric using major traction components from England. 18th September 1993.

Bombardier no. 1971 heads west through Covelinhas with the Pocinho to Vila Nova de Gaia bagged cement empties. 23rd March 2005.

Paul Dorney

English Electric diesels nos. 1448 and 1447 shunt an empty cement train at Pinhão. The train will return to Vila Nova de Gaia later. Note the tile murals decorating the station building. 24th March 2005.

Paul Dorney

A metre gauge Nohab railcar, forming the 19.00 service to Livração, stands at Amarante station. Amarante was the terminus of the Tâmega line from 1990 after the section of line from Amarante to Arco de Baúhle was closed. The line from Livração, on the Douro Valley broad gauge line, to Amarante finally closed in 2009. 24th September 1993.

Henschel 0-4-0T no. E1 of 1922 is plinthed at Régua station. No. E1 was previously the metre gauge station pilot at Régua. 18th September 1993.

Withdrawn metre gauge Henschel 2-4-6-0T no. E202 stands at Régua. A second member of the class is behind. 18th September 1993.

Steam on the metre gauge Corgo line, from Régua to Chaves, ended in the 1970s, but in the 1990s many of the metre gauge 2-4-6-0Ts, that previously worked on the line, were still slowly rusting away next to the dual gauge turntable at the former locomotive depot at Régua. Fortunately, a number of these locomotives have been rescued for preservation. Here, four 2-4-6-0 Mallet tank engines stand next to the turntable at Régua. 18th September 1993.

The metre gauge Corgo line ran from Régua to Chaves. The section from Vila Real to Chaves was closed in 1990, with the remaining section from Régua to Vila Real closing in 2009. A replacement bus service ran for two more years. In this photo of Vila Real station looking north, modern LRV2000 (Series 9500) railcars stand in the platforms. Nine of these railcars were constructed using the chassis of Yugoslav-built, former 9700 series, railcars. Two remain in service, on the Metro de Mirandela, where they are painted green. 12th September 2008.

Paul Dorney

Metre gauge Alsthom Bo-Bo diesel-electric no. 9030 stands at Mirandela with the 14.50 service to Tua. 19th September 1993.

An unidentified Bombardier 1961 class diesel heads west at Tua with the Pocinho to Vila Nova de Gaia cement empties. 6th September 2010.

Paul Dorney

The Sabor line ran from Pocinho, on the broad gauge Douro Valley line, to Duas Igrejas, through rural areas in the north-east of the country. The line was closed in 1988. Twenty two years later, much still remained at Miranda Duas Igrejas station. 2nd September 2010.

Paul Dorney

The section of the broad gauge Douro Valley line from Pocinho to Barca d'Alva closed in 1988. Previously, the line continued to a cross border connection with Spain, but after the Spanish line to the Portuguese border was closed, the line in Portugal was cut back to Barca d'Alva. With the loss of international traffic, the section from Pocinho closed soon after. Twenty years later, the closed Barca d'Alva depot is still standing. 13th September 2008.

Paul Dorney

A metre gauge Nohab diesel-electric railcar, built in 1949, arrives at Livração with a Tâmega line service from Amarante. 24th September 1993.

Vila Real station, on the Corgo line, showing metre gauge Bo-Bo diesel electric locomotive no. 9004, built by Alsthom at Belfort in 1964. The locomotive has been painted in blue heritage livery and is stabled with the historic stock used on a special train for PTG Railtours. A permanent way trolley and its train stand in the platform. 25th March 2006.

Paul Dorney

Metre gauge Alsthom Bo-Bo diesel-electric no. 9022 of 1976 stands at Tua with the 17.50 service from Tua to Mirandela. Eleven of these locomotives were built between 1976 and 1978. 14th July 2001.

Paul Dorney

THE MODERN ERA IN THE PORTO AREA

Drewry Car Co. 0-6-0 no. 1002 at Contumil. Six of these 0-6-0 shunting locomotives were built at Vulcan Foundry in 1948. 19th March 1992.

English Electric no. 1424, in heritage blue livery, stands at Porto São Bento station with the 11.27 train from Régua. 16th July 2001.

Paul Dorney

Contumil depot, near Porto, serviced the English Electric 14XX series locomotives that were used on trains on the Northern and Douro Valley lines. Here, three members of the class, nos. 1429, left, and 1427 on the right, with no. 1441 behind, stand at the depot. A fourth 14XX locomotive is on the main line on the far right. Note the back of the old steam era semi-roundhouse, featured earlier in the book, behind the locomotives. It was demolished later in the 1990s. 19th March 1992.

Bo-Bo electric locomotives nos. 2506 and 2501 head a southbound freight train at Contumil. The 2501 series of locomotives were built by the 50 Hz Groupement, a French consortium led by Alsthom, in 1956/57 and were Portugal's first 25 kV 50 Hz AC electric locomotives. Fifteen of these locomotives were built, nos. 2501 to 2515. 19th March 1992.

Semaphore signals were still in use around Contumil in 1992. Here, a Sorefame stainless steel bodied electric multiple unit is pictured near Contumil locomotive depot, with semaphore signals much in evidence. Sorefame obtained a licence from the Budd Company, USA, in 1953 to build stainless steel bodied railway vehicles in Portugal. 19 March 1992.

Until the closure of the Porto metre gauge system, Famalicão had both metre and broad gauge tracks, with the metre gauge line from Póvoa de Varzim joining there. Today, only the broad gauge lines remain. English Electric Bo-Bo diesel-electric no. 1406, built at Vulcan Foundry in 1967, runs past the old loco shed as it arrives at Famalicão with the 10.20 Porto São Bento to Viana do Castelo. 18th July 2001.

Paul Dorney

A metre gauge diesel-electric multiple unit, built by Sorefame in 1991 with equipment from Henschel & Brown Boveri, arrives at Porto Trindade station. After the closure of the Porto system, these units worked out of Sernada do Vouga. 19th March 1992.

THE MODERN ERA IN CENTRAL PORTUGAL

In the 1990s, Sernada do Vouga was the junction of the metre gauge lines to Espinho and Aveiro. Previously, a third line ran from there to Viseu and on to Santa Comba Dão. In 1993, two Allan railcars of 1954 vintage stand at Sernada do Vouga station. 25th September 1993.

A metre gauge 9400 series diesel multiple unit, built in 1963 and purchased second hand from Yugoslavia in 1981, stands at Sernada do Vouga forming the 12.25 service to Aveiro. 25th September 1993.

Eurosprinter Bo-Bo 25 kV 50 Hz AC electric locomotives nos. 4708 and 4722 stand at Pampilhosa. Twenty five of these locomotives were built by Siemens for CP between 2007 and 2009. 11th September 2009.

Paul Dorney

Two Sorefame 0-6-0 diesel-hydraulic locomotives, nos. 1179 and 1176, shunt a single wagon alongside the shed at Coimbra B station. Thirty six of these locomotives were built by Sorefame under licence from Rolls-Royce "Sentinel" between 1966 and 1967. 18th March 1992.

Bombardier no. 1968 heads south at São Martinho do Porto, on the Lisboa to Figueira da Foz line, with a train of timber empties. 18th March 2008.

Paul Dorney

Bombardier Co-Co diesel-electric no. 1971 stands at Guarda after arriving with the 07.25 Rápido IC service from Lisboa, a journey of just over four hours. The Allan railcar, on the left, has arrived on a service from Covilhã. Thirteen of these locomotives were built by Bombardier, at the former Montreal Locomotive Works, in 1979. 21st March 1992.

An Allan railcar waits at Covilhã to form the 14.00 service to Guarda, a journey of one hour and twelve minutes. 15th September 1996.

MLW no. 1559 shunts the stock of the 15.55 train to Lisboa Santa Apolónia at Covilhã. 15th September 1996.

Sorefame Co-Co diesel-electric locomotive no. 1936 waits for departure time at Covilhã with the 15.15 train to Lisboa Santa Apolónia. Two batches of these locomotives were constructed by Sorefame, under licence from Alsthom, in 1981. They were numbered 1901 to 1913 and 1931 to 1947. There were various differences between the two batches, including the braking systems. The 1901 series of locomotives were intended mainly for freight duties, with a maximum speed of 100 km/h, while the 1931 series were mixed traffic locomotives and could run at 120 km/h. 16th September 1996.

MLW Co-Co diesel-electric locomotive no. 1562 stands at Covilhã at the head of the 15.55 train to Lisboa Santa Apolónia. The Montreal Locomotive Works was a licensee of ALCO-GE until 1969 when the company bought the locomotive designs from ALCO Products Inc., after locomotive production ceased at Schenectady. MLW built twenty of these locomotives, nos. 1551 to 1570, for CP in 1973. They are an export version of a Canadian domestic design. 17th September 1996.

MLW no. 1562 stands at Covilhã, next to the old water crane, after arriving with the 09.00 train from Lisboa Santa Apolónia. 17th September 1996.

Grain silos dominate the scene as MLW diesel-electric no. 1558 leads a second member of the class away from Alcains, on the Covilhã to Castelo Branco line, with a mixed freight for Entroncamento. 13th March 2008.

Paul Dorney

Sorefame Co-Co diesel-electric no. 1943 arrives at Castelo Branco with the 08.03 train from Lisboa Santa Apolónia to Covilhã. 17th September 1996.

Val Brown

MLW no. 1568 heads a southbound mixed freight through Vila Velha de Ródão. 15th September 1996.

MLW diesel-electric no 1558 leads a second locomotive of the same class through Portalegre station, on the Lisboa to Elvas line, with a container train to Elvas and Badajoz in Spain. The disused line to Estremoz, closed earlier in 2009, is in the foreground. 15th September 2009.

Paul Dorney

Sorefame no. 1942 stands at Evora after arriving with a Lisboa Oriente to Evora express. 12th March 2008.

Paul Dorney

RENFE Krauss-Maffei Talgo locomotive no. 2004T, 352-004-6, "Virgen Del Camino" of 1964 stands, with its train of Talgo III stock, between duties at Lisboa Santa Apolónia station. The train arrived from Madrid at 21.10 the previous night, and is scheduled to return to the Spanish capital at 12.15. 21st March 1992.

Opened in 1865, Lisboa Santa Apolónia station is the oldest railway terminus in Portugal. Services to Porto and the north of Portugal, as well as international trains to Spain, commenced their journeys here. Bo-Bo electric locomotive no. 2569 waits for departure time at Lisboa Santa Apolónia station, with the 12.30 train to Guarda. Five 26xx series electrics stand in the centre road. 22nd March 1992.

The 26 km. long Estoril Railway, opened throughout in 1895, runs from Lisboa Cais do Sodré station to Caiscais and was the first railway in Portugal to be electrified. 1500V DC overhead electrification was completed in 1926. North British electric locomotive no. L301 of 1948 stands at Cais do Sodré depot. It was used principally as the depot pilot at this time. 22nd March 1992.

Two 1321 series Co-Co diesel-electric locomotives shunt ballast wagons at Espinho. These locomotives, former Spanish 313 class introduced in 1965, were purchased second hand from Spain from 1989. Some were built by Euskalduna in Spain, under licence from Alco, and others by Alco in Schenectady. November 1993.

Paul Dorney

Two 1321 series diesel-electric locomotives shunt ballast wagons in the yard at Espinho. Espinho is located 22 km. south of Porto on the main line to Lisboa. November 1993.

Paul Dorney

Coimbra B station is located on the Lisboa to Porto main line, 218 km. north of Lisboa Santa Apolónia station. A 2 km. long branch line runs from there to Coimbra station. Here, an Allan railcar runs from the shed into Coimbra B station. 18th March 1992.

A Sorefame electric multiple unit waits for departure time at Coimbra station. 18th March 1992.

Entroncamento is a major railway centre in Portugal. Large railway workshops are located there and it is now home to the new National Railway Museum, built in the style of a steam era roundhouse. Entroncamento is situated 233 km. from Lisboa Santa Apolónia station, on the main line to Porto. Sorefame Bo-Bo electric locomotive no. 2560 stands at the head of a southbound freight train at Entroncamento station. A Nohab diesel railcar stands in the next platform. Twenty of these stainless steel bodied electric locomotives were built by Sorefame between 1963 and 1964. 18th March 1992.

On a rainy September day, MLW Co-Co diesel-electric no. 1561 stands at Covilhã with a train from Lisboa Santa Apolónia. On the left, an Allan railcar waits to depart with the 14.00 to Guarda. 16th September 1996.

MLW no. 1556 heads the 07.50 Covilhã to Lisboa Santa Apolónia near Castelo Branco. 18th September 1996.

MLW Co-Co diesel-electric no. 1568 stands next to the turntable at Castelo Branco with a southbound freight. 14th September 1996.

Sorefame Co-Co diesel-electric no. 1943 arrives at Vila Velha de Ródão with the 15.15 Covilhã to Lisboa Santa Apolónia. 15th September 1996.

RENFE no. 2002T, 352-002-0, "Virgen Peregrina" heads the 12.15 Talgo to Madrid out of Lisboa Santa Apolónia station. 22nd March 1992.

THE MODERN ERA IN SOUTHERN PORTUGAL

Barreiro locomotive depot, situated across the Tagus from Lisboa, was the main locomotive depot for southern Portugal. Here, an impressive array of motive power stands in the semi-roundhouse at Barreiro. The locomotives are, from left to right, English Electric no. 1806, Alco nos. 1524 and 1505, Sorefame no. 1937, Alco no. 1523, English Electric nos. 1802 and 1805, and Alco no.1522. 16th March 1992.

Located next to the works, Barreiro depot was very popular with visiting enthusiasts, who were normally made very welcome. In fact, the friendly attitude of the railway staff was one of the reasons for Portugal's popularity with enthusiasts. Here is a further view of the depot. The locomotives are, from left to right, Sorefame no. 1937, Alco no. 1523, English Electric nos. 1802 and 1805, and Alco no. 1522. 16th March 1992.

English Electric Co-Co diesel-electric no. 1801, built at Vulcan Foundry in 1968, stands at the front of a line of motive power at Barreiro locomotive depot. Behind is an English Electric 14xx series Bo-Bo diesel-electric, a Sorefame 19xx Co-Co and an Alco 15xx AlA-AlA. Ten English Electric Co-Co diesels, nos. 1801 to 1810, based on the British D400 series (Class 50), were built for CP in 1968/69. 16th March 1992.

The body shell of English Electric no. 1809 is stored at Barreiro locomotive depot after a derailment in 1984. Withdrawn Whitcomb diesels stand behind. 20th March 1992.

General Electric no. 1103 with ballast wagons at Barreiro. Introduced in 1949, twelve of these twin engined Bo-Bo diesel-electrics were supplied to CP for shunting and station pilot duties. 20th March 1992.

English Electric no. 1421 heads east at Ferragudo with the 08.53 Lagos to Faro. 3rd November 1999.

Val Brown

The evening sun is low in the sky as Sorefame no. 1938 heads west at Olhão with the 16.20 Vila Real de Santo António to Barreiro. 2nd November 1999.

Val Brown

Sorefame no. 1935 passes Almansil-Nexe with the 08.35 Barreiro to Vila Real de Santo António. 4th November 1999.
Val Brown

Sorefame no. 1938 stands at Vila Real de Santo António with the 16.20 to Barreiro. Vila Real de Santo António is at the end of the main line from Barreiro, next to the Spanish border. 1st November 1999.

Beja is the junction of the lines to Évora and Vendas Novas to the north and Funcheira and the Algarve to the south. Sorefame no. 1223 stands at the head of a container train at Beja. Grain silos can be seen behind the train. Twenty five of these locomotives were constructed by Sorefame between 1961 and 1964. 18th September 1996.

After arriving with the afternoon train from Barreiro, Alco no. 1501 shunts between semaphore signals at Beja. 18th September 1996.
Val Brown

Withdrawn Whitcomb A1A-A1A diesel-electric no. 1311, now preserved at the National Railway Museum, stands at Barreiro locomotive depot. Whitcomb Locomotive Co. built twelve of these locomotives for CP in 1950/1951. They were fitted with two engines, each of 660 hp. All were withdrawn by 1987. 23rd November 1992.

Paul Dorney

Passengers board the CP ferry "Minho" to Barreiro, at Lisboa Terreiro do Paço. "Minho" was built in 1968. 22nd March 1992.

Sorefame no. 1903 (out of sight on the front of the train) heads two coaches off the Vendas Novas line, with no. 1905 on the rear, past the signal box at Pinhal Novo. 20th March 1992.

Alco no.1525 leads the 09.35 Barreiro to Setúbal into Pinhal Novo station. 20th March 1992.

English Electric no. 1805 heads a short freight, from Barreiro to Entroncamento, under the signal gantry at Pinhal Novo. 20th March 1992.

The busy station of Pinhal Novo, sixteen km. from Barreiro on the line to the Algarve, is the junction for the line to Vendas Novas and the north and east of Portugal. English Electric no. 1803 departs from Pinhal Novo with IR870, the 06.30 Vila Real de Santo António to Barreiro. Note the American style signals. 20th March 1992.

With the abandoned line to Montijo on the right, English Electric no. 1465 approaches Pinhal Novo with the 08.45 Barreiro to Setúbal. 20th March 1992.

Sorefame no. 1943 heads a mixed freight for the Vendas Novas line under the signal gantry at the east end of Pinhal Novo station. 20th March 1992.

Near Moita, Sorefame no. 1947 leads English Electric locomotives nos.1429 and 1407 and a single tank wagon towards Barreiro. 20th September 1996.

English Electric diesel-electric locomotive no. 1801 departs from Palmela, past the old loading gauge, with the 17.53 Praias-Sado to Barreiro. 20th September 1996.

With one hundred and twenty km. still to go, Sorefame no. 1935 pauses at São Marcos da Serra with IR871, the 08.35 Barreiro to Vila Real de Santo António. 2nd November 1999.

Sorefame no. 1937 is pictured south of São Marcos da Serra with IR871, the 08.35 Barreiro to Vila Real de Santo António. 5th November 1999.

Sorefame no. 1934 departs from Messines-Alte with IR870, the 07.40 Vila Real de Santo António to Barreiro. 1st November 1999.

English Electric Co-Co diesel-electric no. 1810 of 1969 departs from Tunes, the junction of the lines to Barreiro, Lagos and Vila Real de Santo António, with an express train from Vila Real de Santo António to Barreiro. 28th March 1996.

Paul Dorney

English Electric no. 1810 stands at Tunes with the 16.15 Vila Real de Santo António to Barreiro. Sister locomotive no. 1807, left, waits to follow with a freight. 17th March 1992.

English Electric Bo-Bo no.1422 stands at Albufeira station with a Faro to Tunes train. 6th March 2003.

Paul Dorney

English Electric Co-Co diesel electric no. 1802 nears the end of its long journey, as it passes the small station of Castro Marim, with the daytime express train from Barreiro to Vila Real de Santo António. 27th March 1996.

Paul Dorney

Diesel-electric no. 1336 makes a typical smoky Alco departure from Poceirão, on the Barreiro to Casa Branca line, with a freight from Praias-Sado to Entroncamento. 27th November 1992.

Paul Dorney

Alco AIA-AIA diesel-electric no. 1502 approaches Beja with the 08.20 Barreiro to Beja. Note the French style signal on the right. A goods siding is on the left. 19th September 1996.

Sorefame Bo-Bo diesel-electric no. 1204 departs from Beja with the 06.20 Barreiro to Tunes. 19th September 1996.

A VISIT TO ENTRONCAMENTO

While Portugal modernises its railway, its heritage is also looked after. The National Railway Museum at Entroncamento opened in 2007 with the exhibits housed in a steam era style semi-roundhouse, as can be seen in this general view of the museum. 5th July 2012.

Steve Turner

Allan railcar no. 304 is an exhibit in the railway museum at Entroncamento. Note the front of Alco no. 1501 in silver livery on the left. 12th September 2009.

Paul Dorney

TRAMS IN PORTUGAL

The metre gauge 11.7 km. long Sintra Tramway, from Sintra to Praia das Maçãs, opened in 1904. Today the tramway is a seasonal tourist line. Here, car no. 1 is pictured at Colares, heading for Sintra. 21st September 2007.

Paul Dorney

A Porto street scene, complete with trams. August 1972.
Jackie Green

Vintage tramcars in the streets of Lisboa. 22nd March 1992.

A FINAL LOOK

Sorefame no.1935 stands at the head of a train to Évora at the modern intermodal Lisboa Oriente station, opened in 1998. 20th September 2007.

Paul Dorney

APPENDIX 1: LOCOMOTIVE DETAILS

Broad Gauge Steam Locomotives

Type	Builder	Built	Numbers	In Service 1972
0-4-0T	Hartmann	1881	002	1
2-6-4T	Lisboa, SLM, Henschel.	1916-1944	070-097	22
2-8-4T	Henschel	1925	0181-0190	10
4-6-0	Henschel	1910	281-286	5
4-6-0	Henschel	1913	291-296	6
2-8-0	North British, Schwartzkopf	1912-1921	701-719	11
2-8-0	Schwartzkopf	1913	754	1

Metre Gauge Steam Locomotives

Type	Builder	Built	Numbers
0-4-0T	Henschel	1922	E1
0-6-0T	Hohenzollern	1904	E41
0-6-0T	Esslingen	1889	E51-56
2-6-0T	Esslingen	1886	E81-86
2-6-0T	Decauville, Orenstein & Koppel	1910	E91-97
2-6-0T	Esslingen	1907	E101-103
2-6-0T	Esslingen	1904-1908	E111-114
4-6-0T	Borsig	1908	E121-124
2-8-2T	Henschel	1924	E131-133
2-8-2T	Henschel	1931	E141-144
0-4-4-0T	Henschel	1905	E151-152
0-4-4-0T	Henschel	1905-1908	E161-170
2-4-6-0T	Henschel	1923	E181-182
2-4-6-0T	Henschel	1911-1923	E201-216

Broad Gauge Diesel Locomotives

Type	Builder	Built	Power	Numbers
C	Drewry	1948	147kW at 1200rpm	1001-1006
B	Gaston Moyse	1968	463kW at 1800rpm	1021-1025
B	Gaston Moyse	1955	270kW at 1500rpm	1051-1065
Bo-Bo	General Electric	1949	2 x 141kW at 1000rpm	1101-1112
C	SOREFAME	1966-1967	258kW at 1800rpm	1151-1186
Bo-Bo	SOREFAME	1961-1964	611kW at 1500rpm	1201-1225
A1A-A1A	Whitcomb Locomotive Co	1952	2 x 660hp	1301-1312
Co-Co	Euskalduna/Alco	1965-1967	1007kW at 1100rpm	1321-1328
Bo-Bo	English Electric/SOREFAME	1967-1969	984kW at 850rpm	1401-1467
A1A-A1A	Alco	1948	1618kW at 1025rpm	1501-12/21-25
Co-Co	Montreal Locomotive Works	1973	1615kW at 1050rpm	1551-1570
Co-Co	English Electric	1968-1969	1940kW at 850 rpm	1801-1810
Co-Co	SOREFAME	1981	2200kW	1901-1913
Co-Co	SOREFAME	1981	2200kW	1931-1947
Co-Co	Bombardier	1973	2250kW	1961-1973

Metre Gauge Diesel Locomotives

Type	Builder	Built	Power	Numbers
Bo-Bo	Alsthom/Euskalduna	1959-1967	630kW at 1500rpm	9001-9006
Bo-Bo	Alsthom	1976-1978	740kW at 1500rpm	9021-9031

Broad Gauge Electric Locomotives

Type	Builder	Built	Power	Numbers
Bo-Bo	Alsthom/Henschel	1956-1957	2116kW	2501-2515
Bo-Bo	SOREFAME	1963-1964	2116kW	2551-2570
Bo-Bo	Alsthom	1974	2940kW	2601-2612
Bo-Bo	SOREFAME	1987	2940kW	2621-2629
Bo-Bo	Krauss-Maffei	1993	5600kW	5601-5632
Bo-Bo	Siemens	2009	4684kW	4701-4725

Estoril Line Electric Locomotives

Type	Builder	Built	Numbers
Bo-Bo	North British	1948	L301
Bo-Bo	AEG	1924	L302

Metre gauge Henschel 0-4-4-0T no. E169 heads a northbound train from Porto Trindade away from the Senhora da Hora station stop. 7th August 1972.

APPENDIX 2: RAILWAY ROUTES IN PORTUGAL

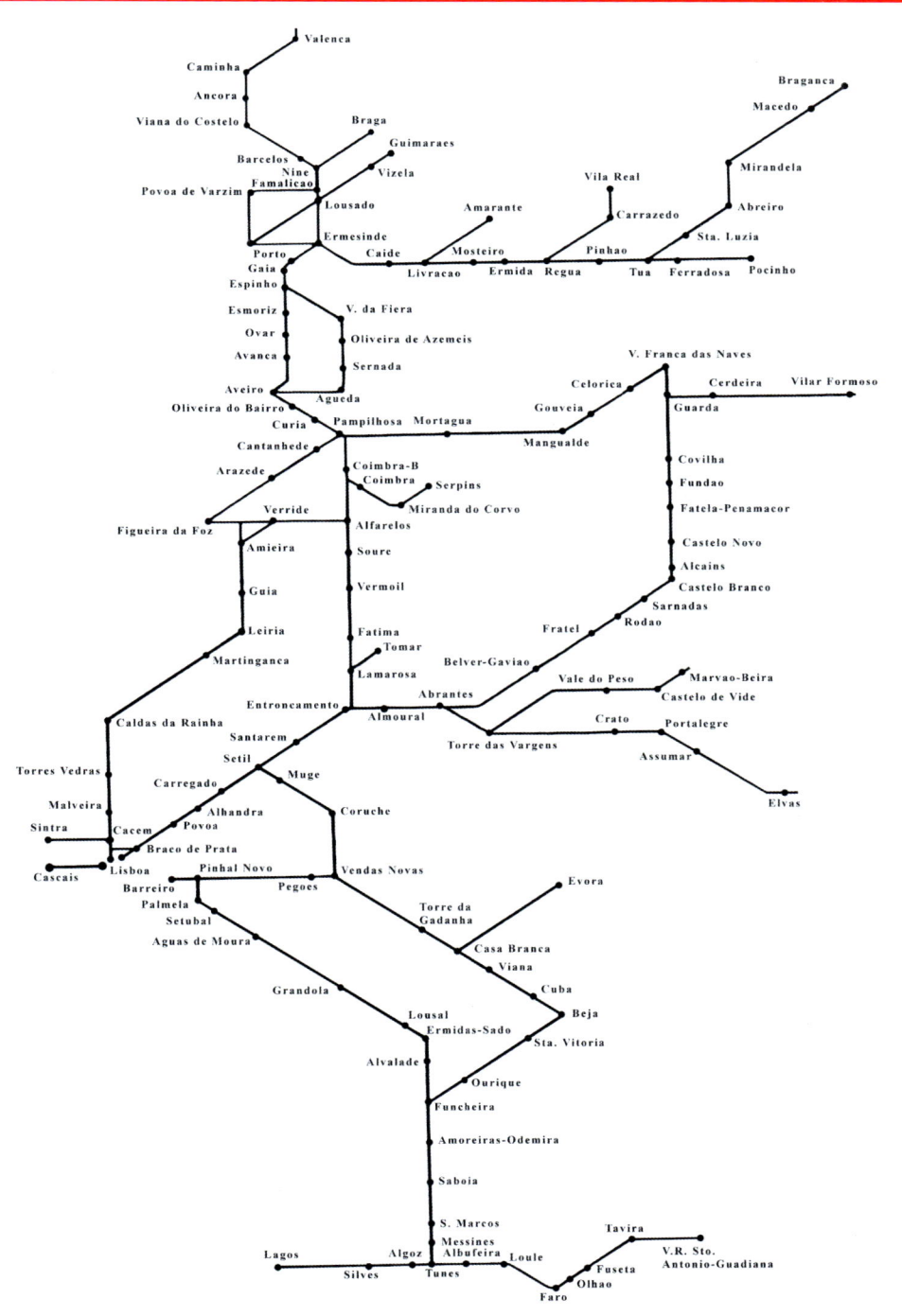

OTHER BOOKS YOU MAY ENJOY!

MAINLINE & MARITIME

PRICES INCLUDE UK P&P

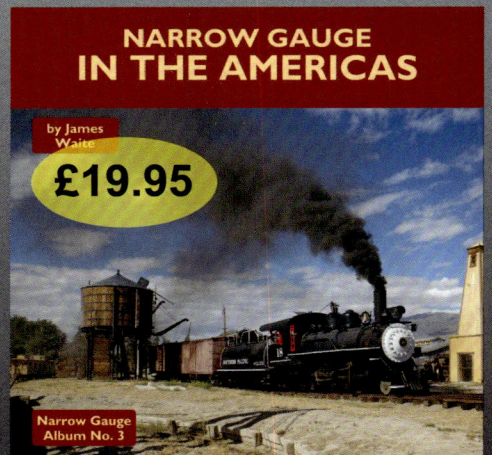

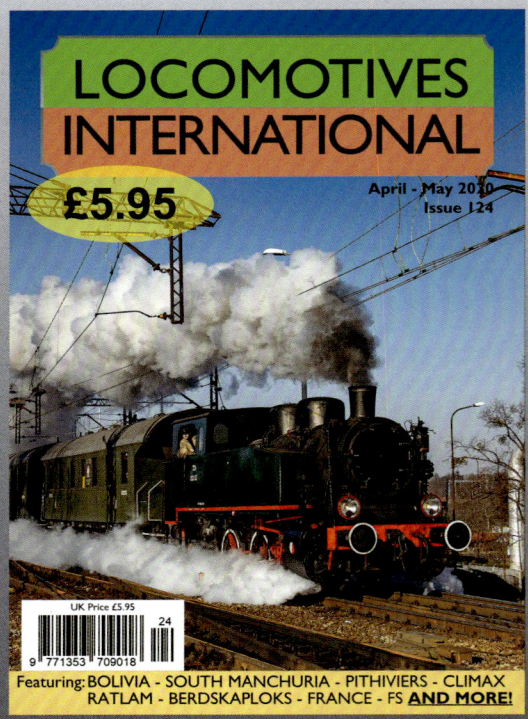

THE SIERRA LEONE GOVERNMENT RAILWAY FROM CREATION TO PRESERVATION
by Helen Ashby
£19.95
Narrow Gauge Album No. 4

LOCOMOTIVES INTERNATIONAL
£5.95
April - May 2020
Issue 124
Featuring: BOLIVIA - SOUTH MANCHURIA - PITHIVIERS - CLIMAX - RATLAM - BERDSKAPLOKS - FRANCE - FS **AND MORE!**

THE AVONTUUR RAILWAY
by Richard Hay
£14.95
South African Two Foot Gauge Railways No. 1

NARROW GAUGE IN THE AMERICAS
by James Waite
£19.95
Narrow Gauge Album No. 3

From the publishers of LOCOMOTIVES INTERNATIONAL magazine

DDR STEAM 40 YEARS AGO
£9.95
International Railway Memories 3
Kevin Hoggett

BY POST: 3 Broadleaze, Upper Seagry, near Chippenham, SN15 5EY
BY PHONE: (+44) 07770 748615 (24 hr answerphone)
ORDER ONLINE AT: www.mainlineandmaritime.co.uk
BY EMAIL / PAYPAL: iain@mainlineandmaritime.co.uk